Chef Mom

Cooking WITH your kids,
FOR your kids!

erin **ALLRED**

The American Pantry Collection ™

Published by:
Apricot Press
Box 98
Nephi, Utah
84648

books@apricotpress.com
www.apricotpress.com

ISBN # 978-1-885027-44-3

Cover Design & Layout by Erin Allred
Printed in the United States of America

Forward

I've always tried to find creative ways to spend time with my 6-year-old son, especially when I can use that time to teach him something new.

I LOVE cooking and one day thought… "Instead of shewing him out when I cook, why not invite him in and let him cook with me!" We'd get to spend that time together and we'd both learn something! A win/win situation, right?

It was just that. We both learned some new recipes, and I learned that my 6-year-old would eat just about ANYTHING, if he prepared it himself! Now, I have just one disclaimer before you get started. Cooking with your kids will take you a little longer to prepare your meals, (hey, the books not called, "Quick Cooking with your Kids" now is it?) but not much, and it's totally worth it!

I hope I can help you discover some new fun dishes your family will eat, but more importantly discover some new fun things about your children (I found that a wooden skewer makes for a great sword fight, especially if the end is weighted with a grape)!

-erin Allred

Ever get stuck for something to do with your kids on a rainy day?

or just want to find ways to spend more quality time together? Why not teach them to cook?

Children love messing up the kitchen, and it's the perfect way to teach them one of the key life skills they'll need as they grow up. And, there's an added bonus, you'll find that even the fussiest of eaters will wolf down something they've chosen the ingredients for, prepared and cooked themselves. But, hold on! Before you run to the kitchen, there are a few things you need to know.

To make your kids feel really special and get excited about cooking, get them set up with their own cooking stuff! Here's how...

Kids' Pint-Size Kitchen Tools

Young chefs cook best with their own personal set of tools.

1. Measuring spoon set
2. Measuring cups: one for dry ingredients and one for wet ingredients
3. Wooden spoon
4. Apron or large t-shirt
5. Pot holders and/or oven mitts
6. Small knife (plastic, paring, or as appropriate for your child)
7. Vegetable peeler
8. Safety scissors
9. Rubber spatula
10. Small cutting board
11. After your young chef has a personal set of equipment, think about providing a permanent place for all these great tools. It can be just about any type of container, as long as it's easily accessible to the child.

Assemble the items first (before deciding on a container), adding any equipment from your own kitchen that you want your child to have (like a melon baller, rolling pin, whisk, or other tools).

Take a deep breath and take the kids Grocery SHOPPING

Especially with very young children, the key is to make cooking fun, letting them choose the ingredients and recipes themselves. As any parent who's battled their way round a super-market with toddlers knows all too well, kids love grabbing stuff from the shelves, and throwing tantrums when they don't get that candy that always seems to be right at their eyelevel. Next time you're at the grocery store, Instead of strapping the little buggers into the cart, try nurturing their inner shopper!

Take your children shopping for ingredients and let them choose stuff from the fruit and veggie section. See what takes their interest, let them choose exotic-looking fruit and veggies they want to try. When you get home, involve them in preparing it. Do little tasting sessions of the stuff they've chosen – the key is getting them enthusiastic and interested, so treat it like a game at first. If you're still having trouble getting up the courage to take that trip to the store, here are some specific ideas that helped me!

Make a List. Make a shopping list with your child. Name each item you need out loud and then write it down. Explain that you have to make a list of what you need so you don't forget anything. Ask for your toddler's help and get him involved.

How Heavy is It? Ask your child to help you weigh fruits and other produce and teach her/him some related words. Your child will also learn about how scales work. As you place the items on the scale, show your child how the arrow moves to show the weight. Remind your child of other experiences with scales. For example, when the nurse weighs them at the doctors office.

Describing Food. Talk out loud to your child as you select items and put them in the cart. Ask your toddler to help. Show him how to place items in the cart.

Checking Out. Invite your toddler to help at the check out. Ask her/him to help you name each item to be sure you got everything. This is a good way to practice any new food names he/she learned. Talk about how you will use the items. This will also help keep their mind off all the goodies that surround them in the check out line.

Food Labels. Help your child choose items by reading the labels on the containers. "We need low-fat milk. Let's see which one says low-fat on the label." Explain that the label also gives nutrition information about the food inside. Show your child the list of ingredients on the label. "This has too much sugar. Let's find one with less sugar in it."

Describing Food. The grocery store is a good place to learn specific names and words that describe things. For example, many children love pasta and there is rigatoni, linguini, macaroni, spaghetti, tortellini, and many more. Talk with your child about what is the same and what is different, using descriptive words. "The spaghetti and linguini are long and skinny compared to the macaroni. The macaroni is like a small tube."

Is It on the List? If your child is old enough to read, let them carry the shopping list as you shop. He/She can read off the names for items you need. If you give her/him a pen, she can also cross items off the list as you put them in the cart.
Turn a trip to the grocery store into a scavenger hunt. Bring pictures of the healthy foods you're planning to buy. The older children can locate the items in the pictures and bring them to the cart, and younger children can use them to identify different foods and colors.

Avoid temptation. Choose a checkout line that has the fewest tempting treats.

Keeping the casualties to a minimum!

Hopefully you made it home from the grocery store in one piece and now it's time to start COOKING!!! But wait, before you fire up the oven, think about safety.

Obviously, if you've got kids as young as three or four messing around in the kitchen, safety is key. It's the same drill as toddler-proofing the house – get down on your hands and knees and look around the kitchen from their level, hey, I never said this would be glamorous!!!!! Are sharp knives and other utensils safely out of reach?

What about potentially hazardous appliances, like hot kettles or coffee grinders?
If you're using the oven, is there any danger of them getting burned?

Are the handles of simmering pots turned inward so they can't be yanked off the stove? Teach children very carefully how to handle a knife, putting them blade-down into the dishwasher, creating a bridge over things you're cutting and walking with the blade pointing away from you."

Never assume that because you know something your child will too – for example, that hot plates can still burn you even after the gas or electricity has been turned off.

Here are some great examples of what children of all ages can safely enjoy doing in the kitchen. Let this be a starting point for you and your kids and I'm sure you'll come up with more great things they can do.

Under 5 years old:

1. Scrub, dip, tear, break, and snap (for example, snapping the ends off green beans)
2. Shake, spread, and cut with a cookie or biscuit cutter
3. Peel (some items), roll, juice, and mash
4. Remove husks from corn
5. Wash vegetables in a colander
6. Measure and pour some ingredients
7. Hand mix

8-10 years olds:

1. Cracking and separating eggs
2. Reading some recipes by themselves
3. Inventing their own easy-to-fix recipes
3. Using the electric mixer (with adult supervision, if needed)
4. Stirring food over the stove (with adult supervision, if needed)
5. Using and reading a candy thermometer (with adult supervision, if needed)
6. Operating a can opener or food processor with safety features
7. Grating cheese
8. Cutting vegetables, fruits, etc. (using a plastic knife or dinner knife)

IT'S time to get up!

Research has shown that children who eat breakfast do better at school – they are not preoccupied with a growling tummy or low blood sugar. Children who start the day with a healthy meal are more likely to have better social interactions, because they are less likely to be irritable and moody. Also, eating breakfast can prevent overeating and decrease the consumption of junk food.

Another benefit – this one more for you – is that once your children have mastered a few recipes, they may likely want to show off their cooking skills and maybe even make there OWN breakfast... GASP! Could you imagine sleeping in every once in a while, (I know, me neither!)

Tips for yummy breakfast success

1. Be patient and take your time. Patience is truly a virtue, especially when eggs get crushed on the counter, cereal dumps on the floor, and the smoke detector goes off because the toaster was turned up too high. Be accepting of the inevitable messes, and plan for a little extra time. You don't want to be freaking out as the bus is rolling up and the kids are covered in flour!

2 Assign cooking tasks. Ask them what they want to do and then tell them it is their "job." "The key for parents is to let their children learn what they like doing." If your child likes to stir, let him stir, then introduce other utensils and their uses when he/she has mastered the task he/she likes.

3. Make it fun. Rename breakfast foods with fun names. Give the kids cookbooks written specifically for kids – these are usually more entertaining than standard cookbooks. You want your children to associate fun with cooking.

Flying French Toast Fingers

Ingredients:
3 eggs
1/4 cup milk
1 tsp. vanilla
Dash ground cinnamon
10 slices whole grain bread, such as whole wheat, honey oat, 7 grain or raisin
2-1/2 cups fruit-flavored sweetened rice cereal

Directions:
1. Preheat oven to 350°F. Beat eggs with milk, vanilla and cinnamon in shallow bowl until well blended.
2. Let kids dip bread slices into egg mixture, then dip into cereal, turning to evenly coat both sides of bread. Gently press cereal into bread to secure. Place on lightly greased baking sheet.
3. Bake 20 min. or until golden brown. Cut each slice into four strips to serve.

My Big Fat Breakfast Pizza

Ingredients:
Pizza Dough (buy the pre-made)
shredded cheese - (your favorite)
eggs
sausage or your favorite breakfast meat

Directions:
NOTE: preheat oven to 350*
1. Whip eggs in a bowl with a little water. Chop up sausages and add to eggs.
2. Mix in shredded cheese.
3. Kids will love to spread pizza dough out on a cookie sheets. Make a small "lip" around the edge of the dough so the mix doesn't run off.
4. Gently pour the eggs, sausage and cheese mix onto the pizza dough. Place in pre-heated oven. Cook for approximately 25 minutes. Dough should be done and eggs thoroughly cooked.

Goldy Locks & the 3 Bears Pancakes

Ingredients
3 cups prepared pancake batter
60 TEDDY GRAHAMS Graham Snacks, any flavor
3 cups cut-up assorted fresh fruit (strawberries, bananas, blueberries) powdered sugar or pancake syrup (optional)

Directions
1. Spoon prepared pancake batter by 1/4-cupfuls onto lightly greased griddle or large skillet.
2. let kids lightly press 5 bears into surface of each pancake.
3. Cook 1 to 2 minutes; turn and cook until golden brown. Repeat using remaining batter and graham snacks.
4. Top each pancake with 1/4 cup fruit. Sprinkle with powdered sugar.

Funky Fruit and Yogurt Parfaits

Parfaits are a perfect way to teach your kids the importance – and fun – of eating a variety of foods. Use a different combination of fruit, flavored yogurts and cereals every time you make this breakfast "dessert."

Ingredients:
1 cup mixed berries or other favorite fruit
1 cup yogurt
1/2 cup crunchy cereal

Directions:
* KIDS CAN DO ENTIRE DISH
1. Fill the bottom of two tall glasses with 1/4 cup fruit.
2. Top each with 1/4 cup yogurt and 2 table-spoons cereal.
3. Repeat with fruit, yogurt and cereal.

"Beary-Berry" Banana Split

Ingredients:
1 small banana, split lengthwise
1 container (6 oz.) strawberry low-fat yogurt
1/4 cup TEDDY GRAHAMS Cinnamon Graham Snacks

Directions
*Kids can do the whole thing!
1. Place bananas in sundae dish or cereal bowl.
2. Top evenly with yogurt and graham snacks. SERVE immediately.

Grab-and-Go Breakfast Sandwich

Ingredients:
1/4 cup cholesterol-free egg product
1   English muffin, split, toasted
1 slice Cheddar cheese
1 slice Turkey Bacon, cooked, cut crosswise in half

Directions
1. Cook egg product in skillet sprayed with cooking spray on medium heat 3 min. or until set, stirring occasionally.
2. Spoon onto muffin half; Let your child cover with Singles, bacon and remaining muffin half.

Stuffed With Stuff French Toast

Ingredients:
4 slices cinnamon raisin bread
4 Tbsp. Cream Cheese Spread
8 slices Shaved Honey Ham
2 eggs
2 Tbsp. milk
2 tsp. sugar
2 Tbsp. pancake syrup

Directions
1. Spread cream cheese spread onto 2 of the bread slices.
2. Top with ham; cover with remaining 2 bread slices. Lightly press edges of sandwich to seal.
3. Beat eggs, milk and sugar with fork in square baking dish until well blended.
4. Kids will love to make a mess dipping sandwiches in egg mixture, turning over to evenly moisten both sides.
5. Spray large nostick skillet with cooking spray; heat on medium heat. Add sandwiches; cook each side until golden brown. Serve with syrup.

Easy Cheesy Frittata

Ingredients
4 whole eggs
4 egg whites
2 Tbsp. water
1 cup KRAFT 2% Milk Shredded Reduced Fat Mozzarella Cheese, divided
1/2 cup chopped seeded tomatoes
2 slices OSCAR MEYER Bacon or OSCAR MEYER Turkey Bacon, crisply cooked, crumbled
1/4 cup chopped fresh basil

Directions
1. Heat oven to 350°F. Beat whole eggs, egg whites and water with whisk in medium bowl until blended.
2. Let kids stir in 1/2 cup cheese, tomatoes, bacon and basil. Pour into greased 9-inch pie plate.
3. Bake 25 min. or until puffed and golden brown. Sprinkle with remaining cheese; bake 5 min. or until melted.

Wiggly Toaster Waffle Sandwich

Ingredients
2 frozen waffles
2 frozen BOCA Meatless Breakfast Links
1 KRAFT 2% Milk Sharp Cheddar Singles
1/4 of a medium apple, thinly sliced
1/2 tsp. cinnamon sugar
1 cup 1% milk

Directions
1. Toast waffles as directed on package. Meanwhile, microwave breakfast links as directed on package.
2. Let your child place 2% Milk Singles on 1 of the waffles. Cover with apple, cinnamon sugar and breakfast links; top with remaining waffle.
3. Cut in half.

Wake-Up Quesadilla

Ingredients

1 frozen BOCA Meatless Breakfast Patty or 2 frozen BOCA Breakfast Links
1 TACO BELL® HOME ORIGINALS® Flour Tortillas
1 Tbsp. PHILADELPHIA Light Cream Cheese Spread
 TACO BELL® HOME ORIGINALS® Thick 'N Chunky Salsa (optional)

Directions

1. Heat breakfast patty as directed on package; coarsely chop patty.
2. Kids love to spread tortilla with cream cheese spread; top with chopped patty. Fold tortilla in half.
3. Cook in nonstick or lightly oiled skillet on medium heat 2 min. on each side or until lightly browned on both sides. Serve with salsa.

COOKING WITHOUT UM... COOKING!

It's a good idea to start with things that don't require heat, like fruit salad. That gets across a basic understanding of how to prepare food safely, how to combine different ingredients, how to get equipment ready, and so on.

Bruschetta is Da Bomb!

Ingredients
3 fresh, ripe Roma tomatoes
4 fresh basil leaves
1 Tsp. fresh oregano leaves (or 1/4 Tsp. dried oregano flakes)
1 Tsp. bottled minced garlic (or 1/4 Tsp. garlic powder),
4 slices sourdough, French or country-style bread, about 1/2-inch thick
1 1/2 Tbsp. extra-virgin olive oil
Salt and pepper to taste

Directions
1. Wash tomatoes. Kids can cut down the middle with a plastic knife, remove most seeds and juice. Chop into small pieces, add to bowl.
2. Tear or chop basil into small pieces, then add to tomatoes in bowl, along with the oregano and garlic.
3. Toast bread slices. Spoon the tomato mixture evenly over toast, sprinkle with salt and pepper. Drizzle about 1 teaspoon olive oil over top of each bread slice.

No-Bake "Dreamsicle" Yogurt Pie

Ingredients
1 9" graham cracker crust shell
1 8oz. container of orange flavored yogurt
1 Cup thawed whipped non-dairy topping
1/2 Cup canned mandarin orange slices -
drained & broken into pieces

Directions
1. Combine yogurt and whipped topping together in a bowl, let kids stir with a spoon.
2. Add mandarin orange slice and stir. Spoon
into the pie shell.
3. Cover with plastic wrap and chill.
Tip: You can also freeze this pie and thaw slightly before serving. Use a black decorating tube
to make a jack-o-lantern face for Halloween.

Funky Fruit Salad

Ingredients:
2 bananas
6 strawberries
2 Kiwi fruit
12 Red grapes
2 eating apples
1/4 pint orange juice

Directions
1. Get kids to slice banana.
2. Kids can wash and slice strawberries and peel and then slice the kiwi fruit.
3. Wash and cut grapes in half.
4. Chop apple you can leave the peel on if you wash the apples.
5. Kids should put all this in a bowl.
6. Pour orange juice over fruit.

Don't be Chicken salad lettuce cups

Ingredients
2 1/2 to 3 Lb. rotisserie chicken
4 medium carrots, shredded
6 scallions (white and light green parts), thinly sliced
Kosher salt and pepper
3 Tbsp. white wine vinegar
2 Tbsp. Dijon mustard
1/2 Cup extra-virgin olive oil
1 head Bibb lettuce, leaves separated

Directions
1. Let child help shred chicken meat with fingers, discarding the skin and bones.
2. In a large bowl, combine chicken, carrots, scallions, 1/2 teaspoon salt, and 1/4 teaspoon pepper.
3. In a small bowl, whisk together vinegar, mustard, oil, 1/4 teaspoon salt, and 1/4 teaspoon pepper.
4. Divide lettuce leaves among individual plates, spoon the chicken salad into lettuce and drizzle with the vinaigrette.

No Bounce, or Bake Peanut Butter Balls

Ingredients
1/2 Cup peanut butter
1/2 Cup honey
1 Cup crushed corn flakes cereal
2 Tbsp. powdered milk
Set corn flakes aside.

Directions
*Kids can do everything
1. Mix all other ingredients well.
2. Roll into balls.
3. Then roll again in Cornflakes until covered.
4. Refrigerate leftovers!! Yummy Snack! Great with milk !

Banana Skinny Dippers

Ingredients
Bananas - cut in chunks
colored sugars
cinnamon sugar
peanut butter
chopped nuts
coconut
ice cream sprinkles
crushed cookies
8 oz chocolate chips

Directions
1. Peel bananas and let kids slice into several pieces with plastic knife.
2. Place chocolate chips in a microwave safe bowl and cook on high until melted - about 1 minute, stirring every 30 seconds until smooth.
3. Let kids dip banana slices in the chocolate, then roll them in other ingredients as desired

BEEP BEEP BEEP...

Kids can use the microwave at a younger age then cooking in the oven. Begin by teaching proper use of the microwave and handling objects taken out of the microwave. Here's some simple things to start off with, especially young children, when learning to "cook" with the microwave!

1. Steamed broccoli and cheese-add a small amount of water less than 1/4 cup with broccoli florets. Place a microwavable plate or plastic wrap over the top of the bowl and cook for 4-5 minutes until broccoli is tender. Sprinkle with Parmesan or other cheese desired and stir.

2. Pop popcorn whether using microwavable popcorn or by placing a 1/4 cup of popcorn kernels in a brown paper bag with 1 Tablespoon oil. Staple shut and pop for several minutes until kernels stop popping. Season with different flavors like cheese or taco.

3. Try various recipes for fondues or hot dips such as pizza dip or artichoke dip.

4. Simple fudge recipes that call for melting chocolate and stirring ingredients together are great for the microwave.

5. Baked apples are another simple and great treat.

And if you're feeling a little more ambitious, but not to much, because it IS the microwave after all!

Microwave Lasagna

Ingredients
1 lb ground beef
1 quart spaghetti sauce
1 (8 oz) box lasagna noodles
1/2 cup water
3 cups mozzarella cheese
1 lb ricotta cheese
1/2 cup parmesan cheese

Directions
1. Brown beef in microwave safe dish (6-7 min on high). Add sauce and water to beef and stir.
2. Cook 5-6 min. Put thin layer of sauce/beef mixture on bottom of microwave safe 9x13 baking dish. Butter dry uncooked noodles with ricotta cheese and place cheese side up on top of sauce.
3. Sprinkle mozzarella on top of Ricotta. Repeat steps 1-3 using more generous layers of sauce until done.
4. Cover with wax paper and place in micro-wave. Cook 10 min. Rotate dish. Cook 10 min.
5. Sprinkle with Parmesan cheese. Cook 15 min. Let stand at least 5 min before slicing.

Mighty Microwave Chocolate Crisp Bars,

Ingredients

1 (12 oz) package semisweet chocolate chips, divided
1 (10 oz) package large marshmallows
1/4 cup butter
5 cups cocoa flavored crisp rice cereal
1 cup mini marshmallows
1 cup milk chocolate chips
1/3 cup peanut butter

Directions

1. Grease a 13" x 9" pan with butter and set aside.
2. In large microwave-safe bowl, place 1/2 cup of the semisweet chocolate chips. Microwave on 50% power for 1 minute.
3. Remove bowl from microwave and add large marshmallows and butter. Microwave on high for 1 minute, then remove and stir.
4. Continue microwaving for 1 minute intervals, stirring between each interval, until the mixture is melted and smooth.

5. Stir in the rice cereal until well blended. Then stir in the mini marshmallows and milk chocolate chips just until blended.

6. Here's the fun part for the kids. Using greased fingers, spread and press into prepared pan.

7. In small microwave-safe bowl, combine remaining 1-1/2 cups semisweet chocolate chips with the peanut butter. Microwave on 50% power for 1 minute.

8. Remove and stir until smooth, microwaving for 30 second intervals, if necessary.

9. Pour melted chocolate over cereal mixture

Hungry Kids Hot Apple Bites

Ingredients
1 apple
cinnamon (optional)
yogurt

Directions
1. Slice the apple in half and cut off the gross bits. Turn it onto its flat side and chop into small pieces (cubed is good).
2. Place in a microwave-proof dish and microwave at 100% for two minutes.
3. Let kids sprinkle with cinnamon if desired. Also, try stirring it into yogurt.
4. Dig in!

Peanut Butterscotch Pretzel Snacks

Ingredients
11 oz butterscotch chips
1/3 cup creamy peanut butter
60 tiny pretzel twists
2-3 Tbsp. sesame seeds, toasted

Directions
1. In a medium microwave safe bowl microwave morsels and peanut butter for 1 minute, Stir.
2. Microwave at additional 10-20 second intervals, stirring until smooth.
3. Kids can dip about 3/4 of one pretzel in butterscotch mixture. Shake off excess.
4. Place on wire rack.
5. Sprinkle lightly with sesame seeds.
6. Repeat with remaining pretzels.
7. If mixture thickens, microwave on medium high power at 10-20 second intervals.
8. Stir until smooth.
9. Refrigerate for 20 minutes or until set.
10. Store in airtight container.

Cheesy Basil Spaghetti O's

Ingredients
1 (15 oz) can spaghetti O's
1 Tbsp. basil
1/4 cup shredded cheese
1 Tsp. pepper
1/4 lb ground beef, cooked (optional)
1/4 lb ground sausage, cooked (optional)

Directions
1. Open up the spaghetti o's and put into a microwave safe bowl.
2. Add basil and meat (if you are using it), cover and heat for 2 minutes.
3. Remove from microwave, stir. Let kids add cheese, cover again and heat for another 1 minute.
4. Add pepper and serve!

Mashed & Mushed Tomater Tots

Ingredients
3 Cups frozen tater tots
3 Tbsp. ketchup

Directions
1. Cook tater tots in microwave till mushy.
2. Add in ketchup.
3. Let kids mush and stir together.

Pack your own lunch

Use some of these great lunch ideas and let the kids pick and pack their own!

Shake & Serve Salad

Ingredients
2 cups torn mixed salad greens
6 each: baby carrots and cherry tomatoes
3 slices Thin Sliced Honey Smoked Turkey Breast, cut into strips
1/4 cup Shredded Reduced Fat Cheddar Cheese
1/4 cup corn chips
2 Tbsp. Light Ranch Reduced Fat Dressing

Directions
1. Place greens, carrots, tomatoes, turkey and cheese in large resealable plastic bag.
2. Place corn chips and dressing in separate plastic bags. Seal all bags. Refrigerate salad and dressing until ready to serve.
3. Add dressing to ingredients in large bag just before serving; seal bag. Kids have fun shaking to mix ingredients. Top with corn chips.

Tuna Dippers

Ingredients
1 can (6 oz.) tuna in water, drained, flaked
2 Tbsp. Light Mayonnaise
14 TRISCUIT Reduced Fat Crackers
10 carrot sticks

Directions
1. Mix tuna with mayo; spoon evenly into two airtight sandwich containers.
2. Wrap crackers in two portions in plastic wrap; place one in each container next to tuna. Cover containers with lids.
3. Pack one container in each of two insulated lunch bags. Add a plastic spoon and small resealable plastic bag filled with 5 carrot sticks to each bag.

Fruit and Nut Wrap

Ingredients
2 Tbsp. Strawberry Cream Cheese Spread
2 Tbsp. raisins
1 flour tortilla (8 inch)
2 Tbsp. Unsalted Peanuts
1/4 cup sliced strawberries

Directions
1. Mix cream cheese spread and raisins until well blended. Spread evenly onto tortilla to within 1/2 inch of edge. Sprinkle with peanuts.
2. Let kids place strawberry slices down center of tortilla; roll up tightly.
3. Serve immediately, or wrap tightly with plastic wrap and refrigerate until ready to serve.

Wrap 'n Roll Tortilla

Ingredients
1 Flour Tortilla
1 slice of cheese
3 slices Turkey Breast
1 lettuce leaf
2 Tbsp. Light Ranch Reduced Fat Dressing

Directions
1. Let kids top tortilla with 2% Milk Singles, turkey and lettuce; roll up tightly. Cut in half; wrap in plastic wrap. Place dressing in small resealable plastic bag.
2. Pack both in insulated lunch bag before heading out the door, or refrigerate until ready to pack up.
3. Serve wrap with dressing for dipping.

Sandwich Puzzle

Ingredients
2 slices whole wheat bread
2 Tbsp. Cream Cheese Spread
1 Tbsp. jam, jelly or preserves

Directions
1. Spread 1 of the bread slices with cream cheese spread. Top with jam; cover with remaining bread slice.
2. Cut sandwich into irregular-shaped pieces to form a puzzle.
3. Place pieces in tightly covered plastic container.
4. Kids can put puzzle together and eat.

Pinwheel Bites

Ingredients
1 slice whole wheat bread, crust removed
1 Tbsp. MIRACLE WHIP Dressing
3 slices Turkey or Chicken Breast
1 slice cheese

Directions
1. Kids will love to flatten bread with rolling pin or drinking glass; spread with dressing.
2. Top with turkey and Singles; roll up tightly. Cut crosswise into four pinwheels.
3. Serve immediately, or stack pinwheels on top of each other; wrap in plastic wrap. Refrigerate until ready to serve.

Broccoli with Cheesey Sauce

Ingredients
16 oz. fresh broccoli
2 Tbsp. butter
2 Tbsp. flour
1 cup milk
1/2 tsp. kosher salt
1/2 tsp. freshly-ground black pepper
1 cup shredded cheddar cheese

Directions
1. Steam broccoli, or place broccoli in a gallon-size zip-top bag, poke a few holes in it, seal and microwave for 1-2 minutes until broccoli is tender.
2. Heat butter in a small saucepan over medium heat.
3. Whisk in flour and cook, stirring continuously for 1 minute.
4. Remove from heat and add milk. Return to heat, add salt and pepper, and stir until the mixture thickens and starts to boil.
5. Turn off heat. Add cheese. Stir until melted. Pour over broccoli.

Butternut Squash Fries

Ingredients
1-1/2 to 2 Lbs. butternut squash
2 Tbsp. olive oil
kosher salt to taste

Directions
1. Preheat oven to 425. Spray a heavy baking sheet with nonstick spray.
2. Peel and seed squash. Kids can do the peeling, under a grown-up's supervision. Have the grown-up cut the squash in half lengthwise. Kids can seed the squash with a spoon.
3. Cut into long, 1/2-inch wide strips, like steak fries.
4. Drizzle olive oil over. Sprinkle with kosher salt. Using your hands, toss the fries to make sure they are evenly coated.
5. Spread fries out in an even layer on the prepared baking sheet. Bake 20 minutes. Using tongs, turn fries over. Bake another 15 minutes.
6. Turn heat down to 200. Bake another 10 to 15 minutes until fries are golden brown.

Monster Mashed Cauliflower

Ingredients
1 large head cauliflower (or 10 oz. cauliflower florets)
2 Lbs. Yukon Gold potatoes, peeled and diced into 1-inch pieces
3 cloves garlic, minced (or 2 Tbsp. minced garlic)
1 Tbsp. butter
1/4 cup whole milk
1/4 cup shredded cheddar cheese

Directions
1. Place cauliflower florets and diced potatoes in a large saucepan. Cover with water by two inches (the water should come up to two inches over the tops of the vegetables in the pot).
2. Bring to a boil and cook 10 to 15 minutes until vegetables are tender when pierced with a fork. Drain in a colander.
3. Return vegetables to the saucepan. Add remaining ingredients. Mash with a potato masher until the mixture reaches the desired consistency.

I WANNA HELP TO!
(ideas for toddlers)

Painted Toast

Ingredients
milk
food coloring
toast

Directions
1. Fill 5 glasses with a 1/4 cup of milk
2. Then take your 5 food colorings and in each glass put 5 drops of food coloring in the milk and stir till color shows.
3. Kids can use a small paint brush and dip the brush into the food coloring. Then take your piece of bread and paint a face or picture of choice on it.
4. Now place your bread into a toaster and wait till the bread is toasted.
5. Butter lightly to give taste

Ants on a Log

Ingredients
Celery Sticks
Peanut butter
Raisins
Butter knife

Directions
1. Remove the ends from celery stalks and cut into 3 or 4 In. long "logs".
2. Spread peanut butter on the celery sticks.
3. Let toddler place raisins on top in a row for your ants.

Alphabet Sandwiches

Ingredients
Alphabet Cereal
Sliced Bread
Peanut Butter, Jam, or Honey

Directions
1. Spread peanut butter, jam or honey on bread.
2. Pour alphabet cereal in a bowl or on a cookie sheet and spread them around.
3. Let your toddler spell his name or other easy word on the bread. Little toddlers can just put random letters on their bread and still have fun.

Mud Balls

Ingredients
1 Cup of peanut butter
1/4 Cup honey
1/2 dry powdered milk
1/2 Cup raisins
crushed graham crackers
chocolate milk powder

Directions
1. Mix all ingredients in a bowl and form into balls.
2. Place a little chocolate milk powder on a plate and let toddler roll the balls around in the powder.
3. These can be refrigerated and eaten for snack later or immediately

Ants in the Sand

Ingredients
2 Graham crackers
Chocolate sprinkles

Directions
1. Place graham crackers in a plastic sandwich bag and crush with a rolling pin.
2. Add a few chocolate sprinkles to make ants, then seal the bag.
3. Give them to the kids to take outside and eat or let them pour it into a small bowl and eat at the table--using their fingers, of course.
Variations: Add raisins (call them beetles), red hots (ladybugs) or mini chocolate chips (spider eggs).

Easy Ice Cream

Ingredients
1 Cup milk
1 Cup whipping cream
1/2 Cup sugar
1/2 Tsp Vanilla
Salt
Large 2 Lb. coffee can with lid
Small 1 Lb. coffee can with lid
Some ice

Directions
1. Freeze coffee cans overnight.
2. Mix milk, cream, and sugar. Put in small coffee can. Place the lid on and put inside of bigger can. Pack ice into larger can around the smaller can and add salt to make super cold.
3. Put lid on can. Let toddler roll back and forth. It usually takes around 15-20 minutes. If ice starts to melt replace with more.
4. You can add bananas, nuts or other fruits etc.

Lady Bugs Cracker

Ingredients
Box of Ritz Crackers
Red Food Coloring
1 Block Cream Cheese, softened
1 Large Box Raisins
1 lb Red Seedless Grapes

Directions
1. Mix 20-40 drops of red food coloring with Cream Cheese.
2. Cover Ritz Crackers with Cream Cheese mixture.
3. Let toddler place 6 raisins on crackers; 3 on each "side" for ladybugs spots.
4. Cut grapes in half longwise for head.

Kindergarten Donuts

Ingredients
1 pkg refrigerated biscuits
1 Cup sugar
1 tsp cinnamon
Vegetable oil

Directions
NOTE: Adult supervision is needed for this recipe!
1. Mix sugar and cinnamon and set aside.
2. Let toddler put a finger through each biscuit to make a very large hole in the center.
3. Heat one-inch deep vegetable oil to 375F in a frying pan.
4. Drop in doughnuts. Cook to a golden brown.
5. Roll in sugar mixture.

Graham Cracker Stoplights

Ingredients
Gramham Crackers
Peanut Butter
Cherry (cut in half)
Orange slice (cut into a circle)
Grape green (cut in half)
Knife
Plate

Directions
1. Spread three circles of peanut butter onto a graham cracker.
2. Let toddler put the cherry on the top for 'stop.' Then place the orange in the middle for 'yield.' And then the grape for 'go.'

MOM... I'm hungry

It's not time for dinner yet, but surprisingly, the kids are standing there letting all the cold air out of the refrigerator, looking for a snack. Every mom has experienced standing behind their child as they peer into a PACKED pantry and say, "There's nothing good to eat!" Include them in "snack making" and you'll never hear those words again... well, hopefully!

Chips & Dip

Ingredients
4 flour tortillas (10 inch)
1 egg white
3/4 Cup fruit-flavored or cocoa sweetened rice cereal
1 container (6 oz.) strawberry low-fat yogurt
1/4 Cup chopped strawberries

Directions
1. Preheat oven to 350°. Place tortillas in single layer on large baking sheet; brush evenly with egg white. Let kids sprinkle each with 3 Tbsp. of the cereal.
2. Bake 10 min. Cool. Cut each tortilla into 12 pieces.
3. Combine yogurt and strawberries in serving bowl. Serve as a dip with the tortilla chips.

Edible Aquarium

Ingredients
3 Pkg (3 oz. each) lemon Jello
1 Pkg (3 oz.) lime Jello
2 1/2 Cups boiling water or apple juice
1 package fruit corners Shark bits chewy fruit snacks, any flavor
8 (8 oz.) clear plastic cups

Directions
1. Dissolve Jello in boiling water. Pour into a rectangular pan, 13 x 12 inches. Refrigerate until firm, approximately 3 hours. Cut into 1 x 1 inch squares.
2. For each aquarium, let kids randomly arrange about 11 cubes and about 8 fruit sharks in the glass.
3. Serve immediately. Cover and refrigerate any remaining Jello cubes up to 4 days.
Makes 8 "aquariums"

Fruit Tacos

Ingredients
1/3 Cup baked coconut
1 Cup strawberries, sliced
1/2 Cup seedless green grapes, halved
1 Medium apple, pared, cored and chopped
1 Small banana, sliced
2 Tbsp. pourable fruit, any flavor (found in jelly section of store)
6 taco shells
1/3 Cup vanilla yogurt

Directions
1. Spread coconut on baking sheet. Toast in 350 oven for 7 to 12 minutes, stirring often.
2. Meanwhile, in medium bowl, stir together strawberries, grapes, apple, banana, and pourable fruit.
3. Fill taco shells evenly with fruit.
4. Top filled tacos evenly with yogurt.
5. Sprinkle with toasted coconut.

Strawberry NILLA Nibbles

Ingredients
4 reduced fat NILLA Wafers
2 Tbsp. thawed whipped topping
2 medium strawberries, halved

Directions
1. Place wafers on small dessert plate.
2. Top each with 1-1/2 tsp. of the whipped topping and 1 strawberry half.
3. Serve immediately.

Animal Chips

Ingredients
1 large flour tortilla
cooking spray
salt

Directions
1. Use animal-shaped cookie cutters to cut shapes from a large flour tortilla.
2. Arrange the animals on a baking sheet, lightly coat them with cooking spray, and sprinkle them with salt.
3. Bake at 350° for 5 to 7 minutes, and your chips are ready for a dip in salsa or guacamole.

Bunny Salad

Ingredients
1 chilled pear half
2 raisins
1 red cinnamon candy
2 blanched almonds
cottage cheese ball

Directions
1. Place the lettuce leaf on a plate. Place the pear upside down on top of it.
2. Using narrow end of the pear for the bunny's face, place 2 raisins for the eyes, 1 red candy for the nose and 2 blanched almonds for the ears. The cottage cheese ball makes the tail.

Banana Dog

Ingredients
Whole-grain hot dog bun
Peanut butter
Wheat germ or sunflower seeds
Banana
Jam

Directions
1. Simply spread a whole-grain hot dog bun with peanut butter, sprinkle with wheat germ or sunflower seeds, and top with a whole, peeled banana and a squiggle of jam. Add a side of milk to round out the meal.
Variation: For a Banana Burrito, substitute a tortilla for the bun.

Fruity Kebobs

Ingredients
1 large red apple, cut into 8 wedges
6 marshmallows
1 small jar of creamy peanut butter
1 large banana, cut into 1-inch slices

Directions
1. To make a kebob, carefully push a skewer through the ingredients, starting with a piece of apple, then a marshmallow, then banana, then another marshmallow.
2. Spread a dollop of peanut butter on top of the marshmallow. Now, skewer a piece of banana and another marshmallow (with more peanut butter) and finish with a piece of apple. Repeat with a second skewer. Makes 2 kebobs.

Sandwich on a Stick

How do you turn a sandwich into a fun snack? Make it a stick-wich!

Ingredients
bread
cheese
lunch meat
grape tomatoes
lettuce
pickles
olive

Directions
1. Cut up cubes of bread, cheese, and lunch meat (we ordered 1/2-inch-thick slices of ham and turkey at the deli counter).
2. Slide the cubes onto a skewer with other foods your child likes, such as a grape tomato, a piece of lettuce, a pickle, or an olive.
3. Set out a side of mayo or mustard for dippin.

Strawberry Mice

Ingredients
Fresh strawberries
Mini chocolate chips
Black decorators' icing
Almond slivers
Toothpick
Red lace licorice
Wedge of Cheese (your choice)

Directions
1. For each mouse, slice a small section from the side of a strawberry so it sits flat.
2. Press a mini chocolate chip into the tip for a nose, using a small dab of icing to secure it in place, if needed.
3. Add icing eyes and stick 2 almond slivers into the top of the berry for ears.
4. For a tail, use a toothpick to carve a small hole in the back of the berry and push the end of a piece of licorice lace into the hole. Serve these berry cute treats with small triangles of cheese.

What's for dinner?

Octopus Dogs

Ingredients
6 Hot dogs
6 Hot dog buns
1 can Chili

Directions
1. About 1" from one end of a hot dog, start a slit in the hot dog that goes vertically to the other end. Turn a quarter turn and make another slit. Keep making slits until you have eight "legs" for the hot dog.
2. Boil and the hot dog will look like an octopus. Serve with head up and legs spread out over an opened hot dog bun that has chili on it.

Oven-Baked Carrot Fries

Ingredients
1 1/2 lbs. carrots
1 tsp. sugar
2 Tbsp. olive oil
1/2 tsp. salt
2 Tbsp. finely chopped pinch of pepper
fresh rosemary

Directions
1. Preheat oven to 425. Line a shallow pan with foil. Using a sharp knife, slice away the tip and end of each carrot; peel each completely. Cut carrots in half cross-wise, then cut length-wise, then cut length-wise again.
2. In a mixing bowl, combine the carrot sticks, oil, rosemary, salt and pepper. Stir till all are evenly coated. Place carrots in pan, spreading sticks out as much as possible. Bake for 20 minutes or until carrots are tender. Serve hot or at room temperature.
Makes 4 servings

Green Spaghetti

Ingredients
1/2 lb. spaghetti
1 medium-small clove garlic
3 packed cups basil leaves
1/8 tsp. salt
1/8 tsp. pepper
1/4 Cup olive oil
1/4 Cup Parmesan cheese

Directions
1. Begin cooking the spaghetti.
2. Take all the basil leaves off the stems. Discard the stems, and put the leaves into the food processor.
3. Smash and peel the garlic. Add it to the basil, and blend.
4. Add the cheese, oil, salt and pepper and blend again until it forms a thick paste (pesto). Transfer the pesto to a bowlful of hot spaghetti and mix well with a fork.

Pepperoni Chicken

Ingredients
1 whole cut up frying chicken (skinned)
4 cups red sauce
3 cups shredded mozzarella
8 oz. sliced pizza pepperoni
2 cloves garlic sliced
1/2 cup Romano or Parmesan cheese
1 green pepper chopped chunky (optional)
1 cup sliced zucchini (optional)

Directions
1. Preheat oven to 350°. In a small roaster sprayed with cooking spray, put 4 tbsp. olive oil, add garlic and chicken pieces meaty side down.
2. Bake covered for 30 minutes.
3. Turn pieces over and put 2 cups sauce on top, then the pepperoni, green pepper and zucchini.
4. Put last 2 cups sauce, Romano and mozzarella on top.
5. Bake covered 30 minutes and 10 minutes uncovered.

Tater Boats

Ingredients
1 medium baked potato
1/8 cup grated cheddar cheese
2 Tbsp. milk
1/2 Tbsp. butter or margarine
Salt and pepper to taste
Extra grated cheddar cheese, carrot sticks, red or yellow pepper

Directions
1. Cut the cooked potato in half lengthwise and scoop the insides into a bowl. Mash in the cheese, milk, butter, salt, and pepper, then spoon the mixture back into the potato skin.
2. Warm for 2 minutes on high in the microwave. Decorate the halves with an extra sprinkle of cheese, then add carrot-stick masts and red- or yellow-pepper sails.

Cheesy Chicken Fingers

Ingredients

12 chicken tenders, or 16 pieces of chicken breast filets cut into fingers
1 stick melted butter
1 1/2 cups of crushed cornflakes
1/2 cup shredded cheddar cheese
Preheat oven to 375 degrees.

Directions

1. Melt butter in a shallow bowl, put coarsely crushed cornflakes into another shallow bowl and mix in cheese.
2. Dip chicken pieces into butter first, then into cornflakes/cheese mixture.
3. Arrange chicken on a baking stone, or in a rectangular baking pan, bake at 375 degrees for about 20 to 30 minutes, until chicken is done.
4. Turn chicken half-way through to ensure even browning. Serves 4 to 6.

Tasty Caterpillar

Ingredients
Store-bought pizza dough
2 white button mushrooms, sliced
Olive oil
Toppings, like carrots, olives, basil, pepperoni
Sauce of your choice, pesto, tomato, (or both)
Mozzarella

Directions
1. Heat oven to 400 Lay parchment paper on a cookie sheet so that it extends slightly beyond each end. If needed, let the dough rise. Divide dough into 15 one-inch balls, combine 3 balls to make the head. Have your child dust hands with flour, then let her/him arrange balls on cookie sheet and flatten slightly with palms.
2. Press mushroom slices under dough for legs. Brush dough and mushrooms with olive oil, bake until crisp around edges, about 10 min.
3. While dough bakes, create caterpillar features from your choice of toppings.
4. Remove cookie sheet from oven. Lift caterpillar off cookie sheet and set on wire rack. When cool enough for your child to touch, let her/him paint the surface with sauce and arrange Mozzarella and toppings. Using the parchment, set the caterpillar back on the cookie sheet, bake until cheese is brown. Cool, slice, serve.

Pizza on a Stick

Ingredients
8 oz. Italian sausage links
2 whole fresh mushrooms, or 1pkg of small button mushrooms
2 Cup whole cherry tomatoes
1 medium onion, cut into 1 inch pieces
1 large green bell pepper, cut into 1 inch pieces
30 slices pepperoni
1 (10 oz) tube refrigerated pizza crust
1 1/2 Cup shredded Mozzarella cheese
1 1/4 Cup pizza sauce, warmed

In a large, non-stick skillet, brown sausages over medium heat until no longer pink; Drain. When cool enough to handle, cut sausage into 20 pieces. On 10 metal or soaked wooden skewers, alternately thread the sausage, vegetables and pepperoni.

Directions
1. Unroll pizza dough onto a lightly floured surface; cut width-wise into 1 inch wide strips. Starting at the pointed end of the prepared skewer, pierce the skewer through one end of the dough strip and press end of dough against end item on skewer. Spiral wrap dough around

skewer, allowing vegetables and meat to peek through. Wrap the remaining end of the dough strip around the skewer above the last item.
2. Repeat with remaining skewers. Arrange kabobs on baking sheet sprayed with non-stick spray.
3. Bake at 400° for 10 to 12 minutes or until vegetables are tender and pizza dough is golden. Immediately sprinkle with cheese, Serve with warmed pizza sauce.

Little Kids' Lasagna

 Set out a table full of fixings (precooked noo-dles, meat, sauce, and cheeses) and let guests build their own customized lasagnas.

Ingredients
1 small aluminum loaf pan (about 3 by 8 inches, preferably with plastic cover) for each guest
1 lb sweet Italian sausage (or ground beef)
1 lb lasagna noodles
1 lb olive oil
1 jar (32-oz.) spaghetti sauce
4 cups shredded mozzarella cheese
2 cups shredded Cheddar cheese
1 cup grated Parmesan cheese
1 cup ricotta cheese
1/4 cup pesto (optional)

Directions
1. Prepare the sausage and the lasagna noo-dles. (You can prepare the noodles the night before.) Remove the sausage from the casing and cook over medium heat, breaking up the clumps, until completely brown. Drain the fat, set the meat in a bowl, and cover with plas-tic when cool. Cook the lasagna noodles ac-cording to the package directions. Rinse the noodles and toss them with olive oil to prevent them from sticking together. (Tip: If the noodles

don't fit in your loaf pans very well, you may want to trim them ahead of time.) Lay the noodles in a 13- by 9- by 2-inch pan and cover with plastic. Then store the precooked ingredients in the refrigerator.

2. Place the sauce, cheeses, and pesto (if desired) into bowls. Set them around the table along with the cooked lasagna noodles and sausage, and loaf pans and serving spoons.

3. Let kids assemble their lasagnas, starting with a layer of sauce on the bottom of their pans (to prevent the noodles from sticking). Have the kids continue layering on noodles, meat, sauce, and cheese until they are satisfied with their lasagnas.

4. Put the pans on cookie sheets and bake at 300 for about 20 minutes, or until the ingredients are warm and the cheeses have melted. Serve the lasagnas slightly cooled and let the kids eat right out of the pans.

Something sweet

Magic Marshmallow Crescent Puffs

Ingredients
1/4 Cup sugar
1 tsp cinnamon
16 jet puffed marshmallows
1/4 Cup margarine
2 can cresecent dinner rolls
Powdered sugar icing
1/4 Cup chopped nuts

Directions
1. Combine sugar and cinnamon. Dip marshmallows in melted margarine, roll in sugar/cinnamon mixture.
2. Wrap crescent roll triangle around each marshmallow and squeeze edges of dough to seal. Dip in margarine; place in muffin pan.
3. Cover with foil and bake at 375 F for 10 to 15 min or until brown. Drizzle with icing.

Easy Soft Pretzels

Ingredients
10 oz package refrigerated pizza dough
1 egg, beaten
1 Tbsp water
Poppy seeds
Sesame seed
Course salt
Garlic or onion salt

Directions
1. Unroll pizza dough onto an 18-inch piece of lightly floured waxed paper. Roll dough into a 16 by 10 inch rectangle. Cut dough lengthwise into 10-1 inch-wide strips. Shape each strip of dough into a circle, overlapping about 4 inches from each end, leaving ends free.
2. Let kids take one end of dough in each hand, twist at the point where the dough over-laps. Lift each end across to the edge of the circle opposite it. Tuck ends under to seal.
3. Place pretzels 1 inch apart on an ungreased baking sheet.
4. Stir together egg and water. Brush pretzels with egg mixture. Sprinkle with sesame seeds, poppy seeds, coarse salt, garlic salt or onion salt. Bake in a 350 oven for 15 to 17 minutes or until golden. Serve warm.

My First Apple Pie

For a time-saver, use a pie crust mix or a ready-made crust.

Ingredients

1 unbaked double pie crust
5 cups apple slices
1/2 cup sugar
1 Tbsp. all-purpose flower
2 tsp. apple pie spice
Juice of 1/2 lemon
2 Tbsp butter

Directions

1. Preheat the oven to 400. Line an 8-inch pie plate with pie dough and trim the edges. Place the apple slices in a large bowl. Add the sugar, flour, apple pie spice and lemon juice, and toss until well combined.
2. Spoon the mixture into the unbaked pie crust and dot with butter. Fold the top crust in half, set it over the fruit, and unfold. Trim then crimp the edges to seal. Cut slits in the crust in a decorative pattern.
3. Bake the pie for 40 minutes or until bubbly and golden brown. Makes 6 servings.

Ice Cream Cone Cupcakes

Ingredients
Ice cream cones - the ones with the flat bottoms
Your favorite cake mix
Your favorite frosting

Directions
1. Fill each ice cream cone with batter.
2. Place cones in a muffin pan. Bake at 300 until golden or cake bounces back when touched.
3. Let cool. Let kids frost and add sprinkles or other goodies and enjoy!!!

Baked Apples

Ingredients
4 cored apples
4 pats butter
maple syrup
water

Directions
1. Place 4 cored apples in a baking dish and put a pat of butter into the center of each one. Drizzle on maple syrup.
2. Pour an inch of water into the dish. Bake at 375 until tender (about 30 minutes). Baste and serve warm.

Dessert Nachos

Ingredients
3 6-inch flour tortillas
Cooking spray
1 1/2 Tbsp. sugar
1 1/2 cups fresh strawberries, cleaned and hulled
1 Tbsp. orange juice
8 oz. vanilla yogurt

1 cup chopped strawberries
1/2 cup shredded coconut or white chocolate shavings

Directions
1. To make the tortilla chips, heat the oven to 350°. Cut the tortillas into triangles, lay them on a baking sheet, and spritz them with cooking spray.
2. Let kids sprinkle 1 Tbsp. of sugar over the tops of the tortillas and bake for 12 minutes or until crisp.
3. For homemade strawberry sauce, combine the strawberries, orange juice, and the remaining 1/2 tablespoon sugar in a blender. Puree the ingredients until smooth.
4. Once the chips have cooled, set them on a plate. To complete the buffet, set out separate bowls containing the strawberry sauce, yogurt, chopped strawberries, and coconut or chocolate shavings. Serves 4 to 6.

Frozen Bananas

Ingredients
3 bananas
6 ice-cream sticks
2 1-1/2 oz. chocolate bars
1 Tbsp. chopped nuts, crispy rice cereal, granola, or shredded coconut (optional)

Directions
1. Peel the bananas and remove any stringy fibers. Cut the bananas in half, widthwise, and push an ice-cream stick through the cut end of each half. Cover them in plastic wrap and freeze for about three hours.
2. Place the chocolate bars in a microwave-proof bowl and cook on high for about 2 minutes, or until the chocolate melts. Check after one minute. Stir in the nuts, cereal, or coconut.
3. Using a butter knife, let kids spread the chocolate mixture over the frozen bananas to coat them completely. Rest the pops on a plate covered with waxed paper and freeze until ready to serve. Makes 6 pops.

IF ALL ELSE FAILS, KEEP THEM OUT OF THE WAY!

Here are some great games to keep your kids busy and close, but not in the way.

KITCHEN "SANDBOX"
Ages: 12 months and up

Oatmeal's not just for breakfast anymore! In fact, a large tub of oats makes a delightful diversion any time of day -- and a worry-free one, since it's fine if an oat or two make their way into your child's mouth. Simply dump a large container of uncooked oats into a lidded plastic bin and add measuring cups, funnels, and scoops -- or some favorite sand toys. When play is done, have your child help sweep up any stray oats, pop the lid back on, and scoot the bin out of the way. For even easier cleanup, set the bin on a beach towel before play begins.

WAITING GAMES eat up some time before dinner with these creative activities.

Dinner Diary: Keep a big blank book and a cup of crayons in your dining area and let kids "log in" with drawings while they wait for dinner. Be sure to date each entry.

Printable Place Mats: Do like kid-friendly res-taurants and print out a stack of coloring-page place mats (go to Family Fun.com/magazine for ours) to keep them busy at the table while you're busy cooking.

EMBRACE THE MESS!

-erin Allred